YOUR

WORDS

COUNT

A WRITING AND EDITING PLANNER TO HELP YOU FINISH YOUR BOOK

COMPILED BY

Lacey Impellizeri

PUBLISHED BY ACORN PUBLISHING LLC

ACORN and the portrayal of an acorn within a circle
are registered trademarks of Acorn Publishing Company, LLC,
Irvine, CA

Words Count
A Writing and Editing Planner to Help You Finish Your Book
First Edition
Copyright © 2019 by Lacey Impellizeri

PRINTED IN THE UNITED STATES OF AMERICA

Cover Design By: Lacey Impellizeri

Digital Formatting and Interior Design By: Lacey Impellizeri

Edited By: Hope Fletcher and Dakota Ellis

Proofreading By: Kenneth Impellizeri

Special Thanks To: Kaya White, Holly Kammier, and Jessica Therrien

www.laceyimpellizeri.com

ISBN: 978-1-947392-71-7

The Title of My Book Is:

_____

Written by The Amazing:

_____

Introduction:

My name is Lacey, and I am your planner compiler person. I, like you, am a writer on my way to becoming disciplined and accountable enough to finish writing a book.

This book is designed to encourage you to move forward no matter what stage of writing you are in. You may have picked this planner because you want to start or have already started writing. The fact that you've bought this planner shows that you have initiative enough to finish your book. I've made this introduction short so you can get to work! Write on! I believe in you!

- Lacey

Before you get started, let's go over how to use this book:

If you've skipped ahead, you'll notice that this planner sets weekly goals rather than monthly or daily goals. I find that with daily planners, if I miss a day I can get discouraged and it becomes easy to follow the path of missing more days. With monthly planners, I tend to procrastinate, which doesn't allow me to build healthy writing habits, and it becomes easier to get behind on the goals I have set.

You don't have to be perfect; every one of us has off days. While we all dream of being full-time writers, the fact is that we all have responsibilities in our lives that take priority, and by the time we're ready to write we've fallen asleep in front of the computer, or legal pad, or cell phone, or whatever it is that we write with. This planner gives you six months to focus on developing habits to help you become a more prolific writer. Focus on writing consistently rather than writing daily, when we break our big goals down it makes them easier to accomplish. Let's say you want to write 50,000 words in six months, that's 2,000 words a week, or 275 words a day. That's less than what's on this page you're reading right now!

(Go ahead, count it.)

But what if I've already started my book?

Fantastic! You're already one step ahead.

You may have noticed there is not a set goal for your word count. That is for YOU to fill in and for YOU to decide. On the next page, I've illustrated the average word count per genre, this can give you some direction as to what your goal will be for the final word count for your book.

Let's say you want to write an 80,000 word Thriller in 6 months. That's 13,333 words a month, 3,000 words a week, or 400 words a day!

Grab an abacus, let's do some math.

I want to write _____ words in six months.

That's _____ per month, _____ per week, and _____ per day.

But what if I've already finished my book?

Then I hope I'm not the first to say congratulations!

If you're like me, the easiest part of the book is writing it (which isn't really that easy). Part of finishing your book is editing it. Most writing trackers gauge your progress on net words written. When you're in the editing phase, your progress may mean you've ended the day with fewer words than when you began the day. This planner tracks your progress by recording the edits you've made in the book, not how many words you've added or removed.

This way you can focus on your progress during your time editing instead of getting sidetracked while looking for synonyms for "said", "very", and "good."

Write on!

What is your goal for your word count?

Fantasy:	90,000 – 125,000 words
*epic fantasy will be much longer, about 180,000 – 200,000 words	
Romance:	50,000 – 90,000 words
*contemporary romance will run about 70,000 – 90,000 words	
Science Fiction:	90,000 – 125,000
Mysteries and Crime:	80,000 – 90,000 words
Thrillers:	70,000 – 90,000 words
Historical:	80,000 – 120,000 words
New Age:	60,000 – 85,000 words
Westerns:	50,000 – 80,000 words
Memoir and Biography:	80,000 – 100,000 words
Narrative nonfiction:	70,000 – 110,000 words
Self-Help and How-to:	40,000 – 60,000 words
Adult books:	80,000 – 125,000 words
YA Books:	70,000 – 125,000 words
* Speculative YA 70,000 – 90,000 words	
Middle Grade:	30,000 – 50,000 words
Children's books:	500 – 600 words

Word Count Goal

This page is blank so you can color in your word count goal!

Tell me about your book:

Title:

Your Author Name:

Genre: | Word Count Goal:

Which chapter are you working on this week?

Short Summary of your Book

What is your Inciting Incident? (The main event that throws the reader into the story?)

One sentence pitch about your book:

What Books are Similar to Yours? (Fans of X would also love my book!)

Character Bio: Main Character

Name:	Age:
Nickname(s):	Sexual Orientation:
Job(s):	Birthplace:
Disposition:	Religion:

General description of their appearance:

Primary Motivators:

Sense of Humor:

Outlook:

Hopes:

Fears:

Flaws:

Why is this person your Main Character?

What is this person's character arc?

Character Bio: *Supporting Character*

Name:	Age:
Nickname(s):	Sexual Orientation:
Job(s):	Birthplace:
Disposition:	Religion:

General description of their appearance:

Primary Motivators:

Sense of Humor:

Outlook:

Hopes:

Fears:

Flaws:

What is this person's character arc?

Character Bio: *Second Supporting Character*

Name:		Age:
Nickname(s):		Sexual Orientation:
Job(s):		Birthplace:
Disposition:		Religion:

General description of their appearance:

Primary Motivators:

Sense of Humor:

Outlook:

Hopes:

Fears:

Flaws:

What is this person's character arc?

Character Bio: Antagonist

Name:	Age:
Nickname(s):	Sexual Orientation:
Job(s):	Birthplace:
Disposition:	Religion:

General description of their appearance:

Primary Motivators:

Sense of Humor:

Outlook:

Hopes:

Fears:

Flaws:

Why is this person your antagonist?

What is this person's character arc?

General Outline of Your Story:

Please take a moment to write an outline for your story. Outlines change so I've left quite a bit of room for you.

Goals:

Five goals for writing:

1. Set a few minutes per day aside to build a consistent writing routine.

2. Get out of the habit of editing as you write.

3. Find a supportive critique group or writing partner.

4. Stop making excuses as to why you don't have time to write.

5. FINISH YOUR BOOK!!!

What is your goal for this book? (Not just to finish!)

Creating a lot of small goals is more effective than one giant goal. Remember to reward yourself after completing each step! Choose something small like a pumpkin spice latte, time to watch Netflix, or something else you love! I reward my progress with fresh French fries.

My small rewards for weekly goals

WRITING

Week 1:

Starting Word Count: _____   Weekly Word Goal: _____

Weekly Focus: _____

Which chapter are you working on this week? _____

What happened in your book this week that moved the plot forward?

What are you reading? How does it remind you of your writing?

_____

_____

_____

Habit tracker

It takes 21 days to develop a habit, and 90 days for it to become a lifestyle change.
Place an X on each day you write for at least five minutes!

M	T	W	T	F	S	S	Word Count	Goal

Weekly Reflection

Final Word Count this week:

Pick one positive from each day you wrote!

What was your biggest accomplishment this week?

Highlights	Challenges

"Sow a thought, reap an action; sow an action, reap a habit; sow a habit, reap a character; sow a character, reap a destiny."

- Stephen Covey; 7 Habits of Highly Effective People

Week 2:

Starting Word Count: Weekly Word Goal:

Weekly Focus:

Which chapter are you working on this week?

What happened in your book this week that moved the plot forward?

How are you addressing your challenges from last week?

Habit tracker
It takes 21 days to develop a habit, and 90 days for it to become a lifestyle change.
Place an X on each day you write for at least five minutes!

M	T	W	T	F	S	S	Word Count	Goal

Weekly Reflection

Final Word Count this week:

Pick one positive from each day you wrote!

What was your biggest accomplishment this week?

Highlights

Challenges

"You don't start out writing good stuff. You start out writing crap and thinking it's good stuff, and then gradually you get better at it. That's why I say one of the most valuable traits is persistence."

— Octavia E. Butler

Week 3:

Starting Word Count: _____   Weekly Word Goal _____

Weekly Focus: _____

Which chapter are you working on this week? _____

Pick one positive from each day you wrote!

_____

_____

_____

_____

_____

It takes 21 days to develop a habit! Have you been writing daily? Write 3 things to make your daily writing habit easier below.

_____

_____

_____

Habit tracker

It takes 21 days to develop a habit, and 90 days for it to become a lifestyle change.
Place an X on each day you write for at least five minutes!

M	T	W	T	F	S	S	Word Count	Goal

Weekly Reflection

Final Word Count this week:

Pick one positive from each day you wrote.

What was your biggest accomplishment this week?

Highlights

Challenges

"You can always edit a bad page. You can't edit a blank page."

- Jodi Picoult

Week 4:

Starting Word Count: .... | Weekly Word Goal ....

Weekly Focus: ....

Which chapter are you working on this week? ....

What happened in your book this week that moved the plot forward?

Need help staying motivated? Try Joining a writing group on Facebook!

Habit tracker
It takes 21 days to develop a habit, and 90 days for it to become a lifestyle change.
Place an X on each day you write for at least five minutes!

M	T	W	T	F	S	S	Word Count	Goal

Weekly Reflection

Final Word Count this week:

Pick one positive from each day you wrote!

What was your biggest accomplishment this week?

Highlights

Challenges

"We can only transform our lives if we sincerely want to. Small changes transform our lives."

- Marie Kondo; The Life Changing Magic of Tidying Up

Week 5:

Starting Word Count: | Weekly Word Goal

Weekly Focus:

Which chapter are you working on this week?

What happened in your book this week that moved the plot forward?

Staying motivated? Tell me 3 favorite things about your antagonist!

Habit tracker
It takes 21 days to develop a habit, and 90 days for it to become a lifestyle change.
Place an X on each day you write for at least five minutes!

M	T	W	T	F	S	S	Word Count	Goal

Weekly Reflection

Final Word Count this week:

Pick one positive from each day you wrote!

What was your biggest accomplishment this week?

Highlights

Challenges

"Proven Fact: You can never finish something you didn't start."

- Sarah Knight; Get your sh*t together

Week 6:

Starting Word Count: _____ | Weekly Word Goal _____

Weekly Focus: _____

Which chapter are you working on this week? _____

What happened in your book this week that moved the plot forward?

_____

_____

_____

_____

Stuck on a chapter? Suddenly turn your book into a dramatic soap opera.

_____

_____

_____

Habit tracker

It takes 21 days to develop a habit, and 90 days for it to become a lifestyle change.
Place an X on each day you write for at least five minutes!

M	T	W	T	F	S	S	Word Count	Goal

Weekly Reflection

Final Word Count this week:

Pick one positive from each day you wrote!

What was your biggest accomplishment this week?

Highlights

Challenges

"You will never always be motivated. You have to learn to be disciplined."

- Unknown

Week 7:

Starting Word Count:	Weekly Word Goal

Weekly Focus:

Which chapter are you working on this week?

What happened in your book this week that moved the plot forward?

I totally believe you can do this! Write one author that YOU believe in.

Habit tracker
It takes 21 days to develop a habit, and 90 days for it to become a lifestyle change.
Place an X on each day you write for at least five minutes!

M	T	W	T	F	S	S	Word Count	Goal

Weekly Reflection

Final Word Count this week:

Pick one positive from each day you wrote!

What was your biggest accomplishment this week?

Highlights

Challenges

"The role of a writer is not to say what we can all say, but what we are unable to say."

- Anais Nin

Week 8:

Starting Word Count: .... | Weekly Word Goal ....

Weekly Focus: ....

Which chapter are you working on this week? ....

What happened in your book this week that moved the plot forward?

....

....

....

....

What books are similar to the one you're writing? Put one or two on your to-read list

....

....

....

Habit tracker
It takes 21 days to develop a habit, and 90 days for it to become a lifestyle change.
Place an X on each day you write for at least five minutes!

M	T	W	T	F	S	S	Word Count	Goal

Weekly Reflection

Final Word Count this week:

Pick one positive from each day you wrote!

What was your biggest accomplishment this week?

Highlights

Challenges

"Mean it. Whatever you have to say, mean it."

- Neil Gaiman

Week 9:

Starting Word Count:	Weekly Word Goal

Weekly Focus:

Which chapter are you working on this week?

What happened in your book this week that moved the plot forward?

Which authors do you notice have writing similar to yours? What do you like about the writing?

Habit tracker
It takes 21 days to develop a habit, and 90 days for it to become a lifestyle change.
Place an X on each day you write for at least five minutes!

M	T	W	T	F	S	S	Word Count	Goal

Weekly Reflection

Final Word Count this week:

Pick one positive from each day you wrote!

What was your biggest accomplishment this week?

Highlights

Challenges

"You have to resign yourself to wasting lots of trees before you write anything really good. That's just how it is. It's like learning an instrument. You've got to be prepared for hitting wrong notes occasionally, or quite a lot. That's just part of the learning process. And read a lot. Reading a lot really helps. Read anything you can get your hands on.

- J.K. Rowling

Week 10:

Starting Word Count: _____ | Weekly Word Goal _____

Weekly Focus: _____

Which chapter are you working on this week? _____

What happened in your book this week that moved the plot forward?

_____

_____

_____

_____

_____

Who is your favorite character this week? What makes you like them so much?

_____

_____

_____

Habit tracker
It takes 21 days to develop a habit, and 90 days for it to become a lifestyle change.
Place an X on each day you write for at least five minutes!

M	T	W	T	F	S	S	Word Count	Goal

Weekly Reflection

Final Word Count this week:

Pick one positive from each day you wrote!

What was your biggest accomplishment this week?

Highlights

Challenges

"If there's a book that you want to read, but it hasn't been written yet, then you must write it."

— Toni Morrison

Week 11:

Starting Word Count: _____ Weekly Word Goal _____

Weekly Focus: _____

Which chapter are you working on this week? _____

What happened in your book this week that moved the plot forward?

_____

_____

_____

_____

_____

What do you like about the characters in the books you're reading about?

_____

_____

_____

Habit tracker
It takes 21 days to develop a habit, and 90 days for it to become a lifestyle change.
Place an X on each day you write for at least five minutes!

M	T	W	T	F	S	S	Word Count	Goal

Weekly Reflection

Final Word Count this week:

Pick one positive from each day you wrote!

What was your biggest accomplishment this week?

Highlights

Challenges

"Substitute 'damn' every time you're inclined to write 'very;' your editor will delete it and the writing will be just as it should be."

- Mark Twain

Week 12:

Starting Word Count: _____ | Weekly Word Goal _____

Weekly Focus: _____

Which chapter are you working on this week? _____

What happened in your book this week that moved the plot forward?

Now is a good time to begin researching Author Marketing.

This week leave this section blank. Instead, start looking into Author Marketing.

You can always visit my website www.laceyimpellizeri.com to read my blogs on Marketing.

Habit tracker

It takes 21 days to develop a habit, and 90 days for it to become a lifestyle change.
Place an X on each day you write for at least five minutes!

M	T	W	T	F	S	S	Word Count	Goal

Weekly Reflection

Final Word Count this week:

Pick one positive from each day you wrote!

What was your biggest accomplishment this week?

Highlights	Challenges

"And by the way, everything in life is writable about if you have the outgoing guts to do it, and the imagination to improvise. The worst enemy to creativity is self-doubt."

— Sylvia Plath, The Unabridged Journals of Sylvia Plath

Week 13:

Starting Word Count:	Weekly Word Goal

Weekly Focus:

Which chapter are you working on this week?

What happened in your book this week that moved the plot forward?

Congrats! It's been 90 days! Write down your writing habits below!

Habit tracker
It takes 21 days to develop a habit, and 90 days for it to become a lifestyle change.
Place an X on each day you write for at least five minutes!

M	T	W	T	F	S	S	Word Count	Goal

Weekly Reflection

Final Word Count this week:

Pick one positive from each day you wrote!

What was your biggest accomplishment this week?

Highlights

Challenges

"No tears in the writer, no tears in the reader. No surprise in the writer, no surprise in the reader."

- Robert Frost

Week 14:

Starting Word Count: .... | Weekly Word Goal ....

Weekly Focus: ....

Which chapter are you working on this week? ....

What happened in your book this week that moved the plot forward?

Do you have a critique group? Pick three friends you'd be comfortable critiquing with.

Habit tracker
It takes 21 days to develop a habit, and 90 days for it to become a lifestyle change.
Place an X on each day you write for at least five minutes!

M	T	W	T	F	S	S	Word Count	Goal

Weekly Reflection

Final Word Count this week:

Pick one positive from each day you wrote!

What was your biggest accomplishment this week?

Highlights

Challenges

"You will never have a greater or lesser dominion than that over yourself...the height of a man's success is gauged by his self-mastery; the depth of his failure by his self-abandonment. ...And this law is the expression of eternal justice. He who cannot establish dominion over himself will have no dominion over others."

- Leonardo da Vinci

Week 15:

Starting Word Count: _____   Weekly Word Goal _____

Weekly Focus: _____

Which chapter are you working on this week? _____

What happened in your book this week that moved the plot forward?

Now that you've researched Author Marketing, write some ideas you have below.

Habit tracker
It takes 21 days to develop a habit, and 90 days for it to become a lifestyle change.
Place an X on each day you write for at least five minutes!

M	T	W	T	F	S	S	Word Count	Goal

Weekly Reflection

Final Word Count this week:

Pick one positive from each day you wrote!

What was your biggest accomplishment this week?

Highlights

Challenges

"Sow a thought, reap an action; sow an action, reap a habit; sow a habit, reap a character; sow a character, reap a destiny."

- Stephen Covey; 7 Habits of Highly Effective People

Week 16:

Starting Word Count: Weekly Word Goal

Weekly Focus:

Which chapter are you working on this week?

What happened in your book this week that moved the plot forward?

Now is a good time to spend five minutes after you write to research author marketing. Write down one blog that you plan to read next week.

Habit tracker
It takes 21 days to develop a habit, and 90 days for it to become a lifestyle change.
Place an X on each day you write for at least five minutes!

M	T	W	T	F	S	S	Word Count	Goal

Weekly Reflection

Final Word Count this week:

Pick one positive from each day you wrote!

What was your biggest accomplishment this week?

Highlights

Challenges

"Don't be satisfied with stories, how things have gone with others. Unfold your own myth."

- Rumi, The Essential Rumi

Week 17:

Starting Word Count: Weekly Word Goal

Weekly Focus:

Which chapter are you working on this week?

What happened in your book this week that moved the plot forward?

Need help learning writing? Consider signing up for a writers' conference. My go to is the Southern California Writers' Conference

Habit tracker
It takes 21 days to develop a habit, and 90 days for it to become a lifestyle change.
Place an X on each day you write for at least five minutes!

M	T	W	T	F	S	S	Word Count	Goal

Weekly Reflection

Final Word Count this week:

Pick one positive from each day you wrote!

What was your biggest accomplishment this week?

Highlights

Challenges

"Imagination is everything. It is the preview of life's coming attractions."

- Albert Einstein

Week 18:

Starting Word Count: _____ Weekly Word Goal _____

Weekly Focus: _____

Which chapter are you working on this week? _____

What happened in your book this week that moved the plot forward?

_____

_____

_____

_____

_____

Don't have a Goodreads.com account? Make one now! (Add me while you're at it!)

_____

_____

Habit tracker
It takes 21 days to develop a habit, and 90 days for it to become a lifestyle change.
Place an X on each day you write for at least five minutes!

M	T	W	T	F	S	S	Word Count	Goal

Weekly Reflection

Final Word Count this week:

Pick one positive from each day you wrote!

What was your biggest accomplishment this week?

Highlights

Challenges

"Learn the rules like a pro, so you can break them like an artist."

- Pablo Picasso

Week 19:

Starting Word Count: _____ | Weekly Word Goal _____

Weekly Focus: _____

Which chapter are you working on this week? _____

What happened in your book this week that moved the plot forward?

_____

_____

_____

_____

_____

What is your goal for next week? How can you achieve it?

_____

_____

_____

_____

Habit tracker

It takes 21 days to develop a habit, and 90 days for it to become a lifestyle change.
Place an X on each day you write for at least five minutes!

M	T	W	T	F	S	S	Word Count	Goal

Weekly Reflection

Final Word Count this week:

Pick one positive from each day you wrote!

What was your biggest accomplishment this week?

Highlights

Challenges

"The chief enemy of creativity is good sense."

- Pablo Picasso

Week 20:

Starting Word Count: | Weekly Word Goal

Weekly Focus:

Which chapter are you working on this week?

What happened in your book this week that moved the plot forward?

Write down the emotions you've felt while writing this week.

Habit tracker
It takes 21 days to develop a habit, and 90 days for it to become a lifestyle change.
Place an X on each day you write for at least five minutes!

M	T	W	T	F	S	S	Word Count	Goal

Weekly Reflection

Final Word Count this week:

Pick one positive from each day you wrote!

What was your biggest accomplishment this week?

Highlights

Challenges

"You can't use up creativity. The more you use, the more you have."

- Maya Angelou

Week 21:

Starting Word Count: _____   Weekly Word Goal _____

Weekly Focus: _____

Which chapter are you working on this week? _____

What happened in your book this week that moved the plot forward?

_____

_____

_____

_____

_____

_____

You're almost done! Are you on track? How does this make you feel and how can you respond to these feelings?

_____

_____

_____

Habit tracker
It takes 21 days to develop a habit, and 90 days for it to become a lifestyle change.
Place an X on each day you write for at least five minutes!

M	T	W	T	F	S	S	Word Count	Goal

Weekly Reflection

Final Word Count this week:

Pick one positive from each day you wrote!

What was your biggest accomplishment this week?

Highlights

Challenges

"We may encounter many defeats but we must not be defeated."

- Maya Angelou

Week 22:

Starting Word Count: | Weekly Word Goal

Weekly Focus:

Which chapter are you working on this week?

What happened in your book this week that moved the plot forward?

Read your challenges from week 1, have you learned from them?

Habit tracker
It takes 21 days to develop a habit, and 90 days for it to become a lifestyle change.
Place an X on each day you write for at least five minutes!

M	T	W	T	F	S	S	Word Count	Goal

Weekly Reflection

Final Word Count this week:

Pick one positive from each day you wrote!

What was your biggest accomplishment this week?

Highlights

Challenges

"Never trust anyone who has not brought a book with them."

- Lemony Snicket

Week 23:

Starting Word Count: Weekly Word Goal

Weekly Focus:

Which chapter are you working on this week?

What happened in your book this week that moved the plot forward?

Are you keeping with your habits? Writing every day? How has this influenced you?

Habit tracker
It takes 21 days to develop a habit, and 90 days for it to become a lifestyle change.
Place an X on each day you write for at least five minutes!

M	T	W	T	F	S	S	Word Count	Goal

Weekly Reflection

Final Word Count this week:

Pick one positive from each day you wrote!

What was your biggest accomplishment this week?

Highlights

Challenges

"The more that you read, the more things you will know. The more that you learn, the more places you'll go."

- Dr. Seuss

Week 24:

Starting Word Count: | Weekly Word Goal

Weekly Focus:

Which chapter are you working on this week?

What happened in your book this week that moved the plot forward?

Have you been encouraging yourself lately? Write a note of encouragement below!

*also, I believe in you! ♡Lacey

Habit tracker
It takes 21 days to develop a habit, and 90 days for it to become a lifestyle change.
Place an X on each day you write for at least five minutes!

M	T	W	T	F	S	S	Word Count	Goal

Weekly Reflection

Final Word Count this week:

Pick one positive from each day you wrote!

What was your biggest accomplishment this week?

Highlights

Challenges

"I kept always two books in my pocket, one to read, one to write in."

- Robert Louis Stevenson

Week 25:

Starting Word Count: Weekly Word Goal

Weekly Focus:

Which chapter are you working on this week?

What happened in your book this week that moved the plot forward?

How has this story influenced you?

Habit tracker

It takes 21 days to develop a habit, and 90 days for it to become a lifestyle change.
Place an X on each day you write for at least five minutes!

M	T	W	T	F	S	S	Word Count	Goal

Weekly Reflection

Final Word Count this week:

Pick one positive from each day you wrote!

What was your biggest accomplishment this week?

Highlights

Challenges

"A goal is not always meant to be reached; it often serves simply as something to aim at."

- Bruce Lee

Week 26:

Starting Word Count: | Weekly Word Goal

Weekly Focus:

Which chapter are you working on this week?

What happened in your book this week that moved the plot forward?

Have you finished? How do you feel?

Habit tracker

It takes 21 days to develop a habit, and 90 days for it to become a lifestyle change.
Place an X on each day you write for at least five minutes!

M	T	W	T	F	S	S	Word Count	Goal

Weekly Reflection

Final Word Count this week:

Pick one positive from each day you wrote!

What was your biggest accomplishment this week?

Highlights

Challenges

"It is good to have an end to journey toward; but it is the journey that matters, in the end."

- Earnest Hemmingway

Congratulations!

If you've made it this far then you've finished your book!
Did you notice that this book was on sale when you bought it?
Yeah, that's so you can grab a drink! On me!

EDITING

You are now in the self-editing phase. Let me be the first to say, "I'm sorry." There's a reason Hemmingway said, "write drunk, edit sober." For many, this is the most difficult part of the process. Don't fret though, you've got this handy dandy planner to help you through editing!

Often, writers look at net word count when they track any kind of progress. While this is helpful for writing, it can be difficult to use total word count for editing goals. Sometimes you can have a negative word total for the day and have made good progress. This one of the reasons I made this planner, to track progress not simply how many words you've added.

Pick goals for your editing. I have a love of "Piece Work," and let me tell you, it is so much better when it comes to editing your novel. Instead of saying "I need to dedicate two hours a day to editing," set a goal for the number of words to edit per week. Not only does this make your goal seem less daunting, but it focuses on progress rather than process.

I'm separating your editing into 15 weeks. If your current book is 80,000 words, divide it by 15 weeks for 5,500 words per week or 760 words per day. For some genres, that may be a whole chapter per day.

Goals:

Five goals for your editing:
1. Set a few minutes a day aside to build a consistent writing routine.
2. Get into the habit of using new words.
3. Trade chapters with a critique group or partner.
4. Learn new techniques and styles you like.
5. Finish your book!

What is your goal for self-editing this book?

Self-Editing your book is an excellent way to get to know yourself as an author. I struggle with self-editing, (so much so that I started this book), so having a journal where I can keep myself accountable holds me to moving forward.

Remember to make rewards for your weekly goals!

Week 1:

Starting Word Count: Weekly Editing Goal::

Weekly Focus:

Which chapter are you working on this week?

Pick one positive from each day you edited!

1

2

3

4

5

6

7

What are your plans for this week that will help you keep track on editing?

Habit tracker

It takes 21 days to develop a habit, and 90 days for it to become a lifestyle change. Place an X on each day you write for at least five minutes!

M	T	W	T	F	S	S	Word Count	Goal

Weekly Reflection

Final Editing Progress:

Pick one positive from each day you wrote!

What was your biggest accomplishment this week?

Highlights

Challenges

"So, the writer who breeds more words than he needs, is making a chore for the reader who reads."

- Dr. Seuss

Week 2:

Starting Word Count: _____ | Weekly Editing Goal: _____

Weekly Focus: _____

Which chapter are you working on this week? _____

Pick one positive from each day you edited!

1 _____

2 _____

3 _____

4 _____

5 _____

6 _____

7 _____

Have you found a critique group? Who are they?

_____

_____

_____

Habit tracker

It takes 21 days to develop a habit, and 90 days for it to become a lifestyle change.
Place an X on each day you write for at least five minutes!

M	T	W	T	F	S	S	Word Count	Goal

Weekly Reflection

Final Editing Progress:

Pick one positive from each day you wrote!

What was your biggest accomplishment this week?

Highlights	Challenges

"Too many words for one book--truth might be stranger than fiction, but it needs a better editor."

- David Benioff, City of Thieves

Week 3:

Starting Word Count: _____ | Weekly Editing Goal: _____

Weekly Focus: _____

Which chapter are you working on this week? _____

Pick one positive from each day you edited!

1
2
3
4
5
6
7

What are words you notice yourself using often? What words can you use instead?

_____

_____

_____

Habit tracker
It takes 21 days to develop a habit, and 90 days for it to become a lifestyle change.
Place an X on each day you write for at least five minutes!

M	T	W	T	F	S	S	Word Count	Goal

Weekly Reflection

Final Editing Progress:

Pick one positive from each day you wrote!

What was your biggest accomplishment this week?

Highlights

Challenges

"The first draft reveals the art; revision reveals the artist."

- Michael Lee

Week 4:

Starting Word Count: | Weekly Editing Goal:

Weekly Focus:

Which chapter are you working on this week?

Pick one positive from each day you edited!

1

2

3

4

5

6

7

Have your characters changed throughout the period of editing?

Habit tracker

It takes 21 days to develop a habit, and 90 days for it to become a lifestyle change.
Place an X on each day you write for at least five minutes!

M	T	W	T	F	S	S	Word Count	Goal

Weekly Reflection

Final Editing Progress:

Pick one positive from each day you wrote!

What was your biggest accomplishment this week?

Highlights

Challenges

"As his editor put it, "Yeah, it's a piece of shit, but it's good shit."

- Margaret Atwood, Stone Mattress: Nine Tales

Week 5:

Starting Word Count: Weekly Editing Goal:

Weekly Focus:

Which chapter are you working on this week?

Pick one positive from each day you edited!

1

2

3

4

5

6

7

How do you plan to stay on track with editing this week?

Habit tracker

It takes 21 days to develop a habit, and 90 days for it to become a lifestyle change.
Place an X on each day you write for at least five minutes!

M	T	W	T	F	S	S	Word Count	Goal

Weekly Reflection

Final Editing Progress:

Pick one positive from each day you wrote!

What was your biggest accomplishment this week?

Highlights

Challenges

"Edit your words, your writing, your sentences and paragraphs... but never your voice."

-Rogena Mitchell-Jones

Week 6:

Starting Word Count:

Weekly Editing Goal:

Weekly Focus:

Which chapter are you working on this week?

Pick one positive from each day you edited!

1

2

3

4

5

6

7

How has your main character changed through your edits?

Habit tracker

It takes 21 days to develop a habit, and 90 days for it to become a lifestyle change.
Place an X on each day you write for at least five minutes!

M	T	W	T	F	S	S	Word Count	Goal

Weekly Reflection

Final Editing Progress:

Pick one positive from each day you wrote!

What was your biggest accomplishment this week?

Highlights	Challenges

"Any book without a mistake in it has had too much money spent on it."

-William Collins

Week 7:

Starting Word Count:
Weekly Editing Goal:

Weekly Focus:

Which chapter are you working on this week?

Pick one positive from each day you edited!

1

2

3

4

5

6

7

What are two of your favorite books on writing? If you don't have any use this space to add books you haven't read.

Habit tracker

It takes 21 days to develop a habit, and 90 days for it to become a lifestyle change.
Place an X on each day you write for at least five minutes!

M	T	W	T	F	S	S	Word Count	Goal

Weekly Reflection

Final Editing Progress:

Pick one positive from each day you wrote!

What was your biggest accomplishment this week?

Highlights

Challenges

"When I'm writing, I make words my b*tch. But when I'm editing, the words make me their b*tch. It all equals out in the end."

– Richard B. Knight

Week 8:

Starting Word Count: _____ | Weekly Editing Goal: _____

Weekly Focus: _____

Which chapter are you working on this week? _____

Pick one positive from each day you edited!

1
2
3
4
5
6
7

What is your target audience for your book? Plan on how you can market to this audience.

_____

_____

_____

Habit tracker
It takes 21 days to develop a habit, and 90 days for it to become a lifestyle change.
Place an X on each day you write for at least five minutes!

M	T	W	T	F	S	S	Word Count	Goal

Weekly Reflection

Final Editing Progress:

Pick one positive from each day you wrote!

What was your biggest accomplishment this week?

Highlights	Challenges

"So, the writer who breeds more words than he needs, is making a chore for the reader who reads."

- Dr. Seuss

Week 9:

Starting Word Count: | Weekly Editing Goal:

Weekly Focus:

Which chapter are you working on this week?

Pick one positive from each day you edited!

1

2

3

4

5

6

7

How are you staying positive while editing your writing? Write words of encouragement!

Habit tracker

It takes 21 days to develop a habit, and 90 days for it to become a lifestyle change.
Place an X on each day you write for at least five minutes!

M	T	W	T	F	S	S	Word Count	Goal

Weekly Reflection

Final Editing Progress:

Pick one positive from each day you wrote!

What was your biggest accomplishment this week?

Highlights

Challenges

"So, the writer who breeds more words than he needs, is making a chore for the reader who reads."

- Dr. Seuss

Week 10:

Starting Word Count: | **Weekly Editing Goal:**

Weekly Focus:

Which chapter are you working on this week?

Pick one positive from each day you edited!

1

2

3

4

5

6

7

What is your book's theme? Does it have greater meaning?

Habit tracker

It takes 21 days to develop a habit, and 90 days for it to become a lifestyle change.
Place an X on each day you write for at least five minutes!

M	T	W	T	F	S	S	Word Count	Goal

Weekly Reflection

Final Editing Progress:

Pick one positive from each day you wrote!

What was your biggest accomplishment this week?

Highlights

Challenges

"I edit my own stories to death. They eventually run and hide from me."

- Jeanne Voelker

Week 11:

Starting Word Count: Weekly Editing Goal:

Weekly Focus:

Which chapter are you working on this week?

Pick one positive from each day you edited!

1

2

3

4

5

6

7

Have you tried Social Media? Try making a Pinterest board for writing this week!

Habit tracker

It takes 21 days to develop a habit, and 90 days for it to become a lifestyle change.
Place an X on each day you write for at least five minutes!

M	T	W	T	F	S	S	Word Count	Goal

Weekly Reflection

Final Editing Progress:

Pick one positive from each day you wrote!

What was your biggest accomplishment this week?

Highlights

Challenges

"Edit your manuscript until your fingers bleed and you have memorized every last word. Then, when you are certain you are on the verge of insanity...edit one more time!"

- CK Webb

Week 12:

Starting Word Count: | Weekly Editing Goal:

Weekly Focus:

Which chapter are you working on this week?

Pick one positive from each day you edited!

1

2

3

4

5

6

7

Do you have your beta readers picked out? Pick three friends to read your book!

Habit tracker
It takes 21 days to develop a habit, and 90 days for it to become a lifestyle change.
Place an X on each day you write for at least five minutes!

M	T	W	T	F	S	S	Word Count	Goal

Weekly Reflection

Final Editing Progress:

Pick one positive from each day you wrote!

What was your biggest accomplishment this week?

Highlights

Challenges

"Writing without revising is the literary equivalent of waltzing gaily out of the house in your underwear."

— Patricia Fuller

Week 13:

Starting Word Count: | Weekly Editing Goal:

Weekly Focus:

Which chapter are you working on this week?

Pick one positive from each day you edited!

1

2

3

4

5

6

7

What is one thing you can do to promote your book on social media?

Habit tracker
It takes 21 days to develop a habit, and 90 days for it to become a lifestyle change.
Place an X on each day you write for at least five minutes!

M	T	W	T	F	S	S	Word Count	Goal

Weekly Reflection

Final Editing Progress:

Pick one positive from each day you wrote!

What was your biggest accomplishment this week?

Highlights

Challenges

"I've found the best way to revise your own work is to pretend that somebody else wrote it and then to rip the living shit out of it."

— Don Roff

Week 14:

Starting Word Count: Weekly Editing Goal:

Weekly Focus:

Which chapter are you working on this week?

Pick one positive from each day you edited!

1

2

3

4

5

6

7

What steps are you taking to prepare your book for an agent/publishing?

Habit tracker

It takes 21 days to develop a habit, and 90 days for it to become a lifestyle change.
Place an X on each day you write for at least five minutes!

M	T	W	T	F	S	S	Word Count	Goal

Weekly Reflection

Final Editing Progress:

Pick one positive from each day you wrote!

What was your biggest accomplishment this week?

Highlights

Challenges

"Put down everything that comes into your head and then you're a writer. But an author is one who can judge his own stuff's worth, without pity, and destroy most of it."

- Colette (*Casual Chance*, 1964)"

Week 15:

Starting Word Count: Weekly Editing Goal:

Weekly Focus:

Which chapter are you working on this week?

Pick one positive from each day you edited!

1

2

3

4

5

6

7

You're almost done! What are you doing to celebrate?

Habit tracker
It takes 21 days to develop a habit, and 90 days for it to become a lifestyle change.
Place an X on each day you write for at least five minutes!

M	T	W	T	F	S	S	Word Count	Goal

Weekly Reflection

Final Editing Progress:

Pick one positive from each day you wrote!

What was your biggest accomplishment this week?

Highlights

Challenges

"Kill your darlings, kill your darlings, even when it breaks your egocentric little scribbler's heart, kill your darlings."

- Stephen King

NOW WHAT?

You did it!

Congratulations. You have now officially completed your book! I knew you could do it. You're probably now asking yourself the age-old question, "Now What?" Let me give you a rundown on some steps you can take now that you have officially completed your book.

Find Beta Readers

Beta Readers are people you know and trust who will read your book for you and give you unbiased feedback of how they felt about it. Your beta readers will read your book and point out any larger changes you may want to make before sending it out to an agent or editor.

Find an Editor

You just spent 15 weeks editing this f*cker on your own. But now that you've found beta readers who have probably gone in and found the bigger plot holes in your novel, you need somebody with fresher eyes than you to go in and find the things you may have missed.

Write a good Query Letter and Synopsis of your book.

A Query Letter is an introduction of yourself and your work that you send to an agent. It will include a little bit about yourself and about your work. If an agent is interested in you from a query, they may ask for a synopsis.

A synopsis is a brief summary of your book from beginning to end. An agent or publisher will ask for your synopsis, to better understand what happens in your book.

Get prepared for Rejection.

This is a brutal industry. Before you start submitting, be prepared for rejection. Good books every year are rejected by publishers only to become best sellers and major motion pictures later in life.

Still Alice by Lisa Genova	Rejected 100 times
The Thomas Berryman Number by James Patterson	Rejected 31 times
John Crow's Devil by Marlon James	Rejected 78 times
The Help by Kathryn Stockett	Rejected 60 times
Chicken Soup for the Soul	Rejected 144 times
Carrie by Stephen King	Rejected 30 times

Educate yourself on the different kinds of publishing companies.

Before you begin the querying process, it's important to educate yourself on the different types of publishing (Traditional, small press, hybrid, and self-publishing). Be sure to educate yourself and find the type of publishing that works best for you and your story.

Query Your Book to Agents

Once you've edited our book and have written a query, you're ready to get up and send your book to agents. The literary industry changes so fast. If you want up-to-date information on selling your book, then please check out my website www.laceyimpellizeri.com for daily updates on the industry.

NOTES:

The Literary Industry Changes So Fast:

If you want up-to-date information about writing, marketing, and

publishing, be sure to check out my website at

www.laceyimpellizeri.com

I'm an independent Marketing Manager for Authors with experience in

book design, art, Marketing, Website Design, and Personal Branding.

If you have any questions just email me at lacey@laceyimpellizeri.com

Made in the USA
Las Vegas, NV
07 August 2021